MOTIVATION -
THE FIRE WITHIN

DON WALKER

authorHOUSE®

AuthorHouse™
1663 Liberty Drive
Bloomington, IN 47403
www.authorhouse.com
Phone: 1 (800) 839-8640

Published by AuthorHouse 09/03/2019

ISBN: 978-1-7283-2578-1 (sc)
ISBN: 978-1-7283-2576-7 (hc)
ISBN: 978-1-7283-2577-4 (e)

Library of Congress Control Number: 2019913081

Print information available on the last page.

*Scripture quotations marked NIV are taken from the Holy Bible, New
International Version®. NIV®. Copyright © 1973, 1978, 1984 by International
Bible Society. Used by permission of Zondervan. All rights reserved. [Biblica]*

*Scripture quotations marked NASB are taken from the New American
Standard Bible®, Copyright © 1960, 1962, 1963, 1968, 1971, 1972, 1973,
1975, 1977, 1995 by The Lockman Foundation. Used by permission.*

*Scripture quotations marked NKJV are taken from the New King James Version.
Copyright © 1982 by Thomas Nelson, Inc. Used by permission. All rights reserved.*

This book is printed on acid-free paper.

DEDICATION PAGE

This book is dedicated to my parents,

Iteria and Lester Walker with love

BEFORE YOU ENTER

This book is a gateway to a simple journey to motivation, and discovering the fire within you, laid out in three parts.

1. The introductory portion unpacked my own journey of why I don't have any quit in me, why I don't fear, and why my routine includes discipline with a purpose. Read this section and you will see yourself on the page.

2. The second portion contains six chapters on unleashing self-motivation – the path that is necessary for all of us. Like a good team that builds on fundamentals, together they create

a whole program that must be experienced to become a champion.

3. The last portion of the book contains five chapters on uncovering a position to receive what God has in store for you. As you read this section notice how the first section was preparation for the second.

Bible: NIV, NASB, NKJV

Editor: Cynthia Lacey Hood

Co-editor: Mallory Smith

INTRODUCTION

"And we know that all things work
together for good to them that love God,
to them who are the called according to
his purpose." ~Romans 8:28 KJV

"The fire that lives within," that statement changed my outlook on life and my circumstances. My life changed drastically when I allowed my conscience to align with God's purpose for my life. When I allowed God to take the wheel and drive in my life, things started to make sense. After reading this book, my hope and prayer is that you will be motivated to change your mentality, conquer your dreams, and allow God to become your source for every desire of your heart. Once you allow God to become your source, the mountains in your life will cease to exist. You will walk in authority by knowing your assignment (purpose). In other words, you will be reigniting the fire that has always been living within.

It has taken me 10 years to ignite the fire within and accept my God-given Gifts. My gifts were not like my surroundings so I battled to be like my peers in order to be accepted. Therefore I battled every day with flesh and blood looking for a change, and the change never happened. I had a routine that produced the same results every year and every year I said that it would be different. I was writing books, and motivational speeches, but I wasn't' completing them and no one was reading them but me. One morning when I awoke, I started my regular routine devotion and reading. This particular morning I picked up my own book and started reading it. I couldn't put it down - it was motivating. I realized at that moment that there was (Fire Within) and I asked, "Where did it go." The Spirit said, "Nowhere, it is dormant, you still have it." As mentioned above, that changed my outlook. I had to change my routine into a discipline with a purpose. I thought of the Apostle Paul in the book of Philippians when he said, "Being confident of this very thing that He who has begun a good work in you will complete it until the day of Jesus Christ." My fire was shut down because of disappointments, not realizing how disappointments had affected my outlook. Without fire, I was hiding out expecting something to happen without effort and without participation. In others words, I was sitting on my gifts from God not wanting to be seen nor heard because of disappointments.

I knew that it was something on the inside of me that kept me working when it looked like I was losing. Why didn't I quit? It was the fire within that held me together. When I wanted to quit the fire reminded me why I was fighting. As Apostle Paul told Timothy in the book of II Timothy, "Therefore I remind you to stir up the gift of God which is in you through the laying on of my hands. For God has not given us a spirit of fear, but of power and of love and of a sound mind." The Fire Within reminded me why I shouldn't quit, and why I shouldn't fear. I hope you get the idea of why you shouldn't quit, and why your routine should be discipline with a purpose. In the book Romans it says, "And we know that all things work together for good to them that love God, to them who are called according to his purpose." I hope this book motivates you to develop discipline with a purpose in every aspect of your life.

CONTENTS

CONTENTS

CHAPTER 1

Motivating Yourself

ou may ask yourself, "How can I motivate myself?" A friend of mine asked me, "Is it possible to motivate myself when I have bills and other responsibilities in my life?" Well, the answer is yes, you can achieve motivation and you deserve it! It does not matter about your constant responsibilities and other things that are trying to divert your attention. This opportunity is ultimately about you getting into God's purpose for your life. Trials and tribulations are going to take place in your life, but life goes on and time continues to pass you by. At the end of the day it's all about staying motivated and experiencing your God-given purpose.

Let me elaborate: When I was in high school, playing basketball was my life. My stature did not meet the NBA standards, but my heart and my talent were unquestionable. My heart and my talent made room for me and allowed me to have friends who were older and extraordinary. My friends don't know this, but I would like to give them a piece of my mind. I say that because I missed what they were trying to teach me. I know that teaching me was never their intention, but now I know I should have been getting into my purpose. They had a mentality that oozed motivation in high school. When I think back to Saturday nights, I never saw them hanging out and I never heard about them getting into trouble. Whenever their names were mentioned, it was about good grades and achieving in school. On Sunday mornings, I would arrive to church around 11:45 a.m., just in time to hear the sermon and I would leave shortly after to watch the NFL or NBA game. After that, I would play basketball for the remainder of the evening.

I never participated in church events or outreach; I would not even recite an Easter speech. When I did hear about things that had taken place in church, it would be from my mom and aunt. Now, I understand better that I should have been paying more attention to my friends and the way they conducted themselves. Even my brother would always say, "You don't have to go to church, just go to Mom's house on Monday?" That makes me smile at how true that statement is.

Now, I am a pastor and I find myself reflecting on my life. I think about how my friends were always at church at 9:00 a.m. sharp. Even though, I would arrive to church at 11:45 a.m. and leave shortly after, my friends were still there. They were very active in church activities and attending church events. I was not active in church nor was I active in high school activities; I was walking around with no motivation or purpose; just barely doing enough to get by.

My friends were motivated to be something spectacular. They were using their motivation as fuel to obtain their purpose. They knew that doing good in high school and participating in church were going to be referrals for their future. Participation shows your ability and your effort; the key thing being your effort. When there is effort, your intellect will be developed because effort disables fear.

In high school my friends were fearless; they participated in Student Government Association, choir, debate team, honor society, and every sport they could play. Today, they have been more successful because they developed a purpose early in their life. They went to college with a purpose and God led them right into their destiny. Now, do you understand why I want to give them a piece of my mind? To let them know that I got it and I realize that participation is a key to your motivation and obtaining your purpose in life.

My talent and my heart got me connected to my purpose; but I didn't get it then because I didn't participate. It is so important that you start participating in something today that will fuel your motivation into your future, develop your purpose and remove your fears in life. When your fear is replaced with determination and the overall will to succeed, your focus can't be confused. The Apostle Paul said to the Philippians, "Being confident of this very thing, that He which hath begun a good work in you will perform it until the day of Jesus Christ' (Philippians 1:6 KJV). This is referring to you today. All you must do is participate and the Lord will perform a work in you that you could never imagine. Remember, effort is key.

If you could talk to my friends today, I know they would say, "Participation is one of the keys to reigniting the fire of motivation in yourself!" If you do it, prepare for provisions to be made for you as you walk into your destiny.

CHAPTER 2

Define Who You Are and What You Stand For

n this life, I'm positive that you have had numerous experiences ranging from good to bad, to just plain old ugly. But that's normal because that's life. Ultimately, you must learn something from every situation that you lived through. You must carry with you the things that you have learned in church, school, work, personal life, and growing up and put those things in action as you travel this journey we call life. Do not allow your living conditions or your income stop you.

I told my co-workers one day that I stay motivated and that I shop off the wood. Whenever you visit the mall, go into a store such as Belk, Macy's, or JCPenney's and look at the merchandise that is on wood shelving. Then ask the customer service representative does that merchandise ever go on sale. My co-workers looked at me funny and I noticed their face was filled with pure confusion. Reading their facial gestures looked as if they were saying,

"I know how much you make because I work here, too." The point I'm making is that my job does not define anything about me and that I was getting ready to take my ministry to the next level. At that very moment, I refused to lack motivation in my life regardless of the things that would come up against me.

The same week, I started being on time for my meetings; I ensured my clothes were ready the night before my scheduled shift; I started praying at 4:30 a.m., 12 noon, and before going to bed. I also developed a program called *Uplift Thursday* to motivate others to bring the best out of themselves. I no longer needed validation from "man" to preach, serve, or praise God. I was willing to go up against any evil entity. There was no longer such thing as the word "No." I walked as if I had never been hurt. I didn't allow money to define me because God is my source.

"God knows that you will have need of all things, but seek first the Kingdom of God, and His righteousness, and all these things shall be added unto you," (Matthew 6:32-33 NKJV). Seek the Kingdom of God and you will be defined by God and not the things of the world. Make up your mind that you are willing to fight for your identity in the Lord. When you take one step the Lord will take two. When I started putting my faith in God first, everything in my life started to happen. Did you notice I said my faith in God?

God has never lost, He has never given up, and He is always on time. I had to be on a winning team. When God showed me my position on His team, I knew I couldn't lose. The Apostle Paul knew he could not lose when he was defined by Jesus. You are not going to lose when you allow yourself to be defined by the word and stay motivated through all trials and tribulations.

CHAPTER 3

Recognize the Purpose of Your Talent

Honestly, most people think they are where they are because of luck or their talent alone. Well, I have some news for you. That is so far from the truth. It is not about your talents alone. It is about your ability to get and stay motivated. There is so much talent in our churches, local parks and weight rooms because people are not willing to share their personal motivation. I always hear people talking about their talents, but they fail to take a deeper look.

The church pews are full of the next Yolanda Adams and T.D. Jakes, while our gyms are full of the next Michael Jordan or Stephen Curry and our weight rooms are jam-packed with the next Dewayne Johnson (Rock). Talent is not hard to find, but finding someone who has recognized the purpose of their talent is difficult. The Apostle Paul stated, "Every man hath his proper gift of God, one after this manner, and another after that." (1 Corinthians 7:7 KJV). It is so easy to imitate the names that I mentioned above. Do not be led by your talents, allow God to lead you.

Now, have you asked yourself how do you become respectful and motivated enough to take yourself to the next level? Respect comes when you recognize that you have what it takes to keep moving forward. Motivation comes when you learn more about your specific talents and you are ready to let your fire burn without fault. When you are willing to become a student and learn more about your talent, you will get the respect. This motivation will help you realize that God gave you the talent for His purpose and not your purpose. What God has in mind for your life and what you have in mind for your life may be two totally different things. But, just remember that God always has your best interest in mind.

Respect and motivation will make you "recognize the purpose of your talent." You must live a life of motivation so that others can benefit from what they see in you. Let God use your talent for His purpose, and He will make room for you.

Also, your attitude must change for you to gain respect. Every morning that you get up, start preparing for your next level. Why? Because you have no idea who God could place in your path on that very day. The locations are endless; it could be in traffic, a grocery store, gas station, or your favorite restaurant. The things that God has planned for your life, no one can stop. So, you've got to stay motivated for when He places that next CEO of a company in front of you, you will make a wondrous first impression.

Always be in the purpose of your talent because everyone you meet could be an opportunity to that could take you to your next level. Also, God can place His people in your path to unlock unforeseen potential in you. In a lot of cases, others can see your potential and successes before you do. So don't get caught slipping.

CHAPTER 4

Recognize God as Your Source

know most people feel like it is too late for them. Well, I'm here to tell you it is never too late to be great. Each day is brand new and that is another opportunity to do better than you did the day before. "Let your conversation be without covetousness; and be content with such things as ye have; for He hath said, I will never leave thee, nor forsake thee," (Hebrew 13:5 KJV). You must renew your mind to know without a shadow of a doubt that it is never too late.

After getting a job, our first thought is to pay bills. We forget about living from one day to the next. Today you must develop the mindset that your bills are already paid and trust in God that it is done. I have a friend who told me that he worked all week and was immensely disappointed when he picked up his check. So I reminded him about the poor widow in the scripture who gave two cents and Jesus said that she had put more in than them all; He bragged on her (Luke 21:1-4 NKJ). The two cents to the widow meant a great deal to her livelihood and she did not have extra to give. At that moment, I told him that he must recognize God as his Source. I told him to be obedient, to tithe, and to make a habit of sowing a seed once a month.

While talking with him I discovered that the job was not the problem. The problem was he did not recognize God as his source. Inside this young man lived a dream and he was not pursuing it. He was settling in life and not even realizing it. It was causing him frustration and confusion on his job and in his personal life. His dream was to attend fire college and become a fireman. I told him these words: Walk like you have never been hurt.

Have you stopped pursuing your dreams? Have you put your dreams on hold? Your fire within is your motivation. The fire that is lit within you is a reminder of your dreams, ambition, and all the things you said you would not forget. After speaking with my friend, he realized that he had not been recognizing God as his source and that it was time to realize where "all things" come from. The young man had already taken and passed the test for fire college and all that was left to do was wait on God. He started living as if his current job was a referral for his dream job. The following week, he started tithing regularly and sowing seeds in the ministry and community and became an active mentor to the young men in church. The referral for fire college that he had been praying for came through, but he did not have enough money to pay for his classes. Then we saw the Lord intervene and provide. God's timing is perfect.

But let us not be mistaken. This young man prayed diligently and continued with life as if it was already done. He did not know how it was going to be done, but he had faith that God was going to work it out in his best interest. God did it and all the praise and glory goes to Him.

As of today, he has started fire college in Tuscaloosa, Alabama because he recognizes God as his source. So this brings me back to the realization of the walk and allowing God to be your Source. Most of us have been hurt by something or someone that led to frustration and confusion because we are out of place with God. When you are not pursuing your dreams and taking advantage of the gifts that God has placed in your heart; frustration can set in.

The soulful artist Al Green stated in a song, "How can a loser ever win?" I have realized that a lot of my peers feel like losers because they have stopped pursuing their dreams. They are present every Sunday for church, but they are experiencing frustration and feeling as if they just cannot continue. The devil is a lie, you can make it! "God is not the author of confusion, but of peace, as in all churches of the saints,"

(1 Corinthians 14:33 NKJV). Are you listening and receiving these words with your heart right now?

Have you ever heard a man say that if you do not get right with God you are going to hell? I know your first thought is probably, "Well, that is what I am trying to do by being in church is get right." I want you to know that is far from the truth. Our God is all about love, patience, kindness, peace, and joy. He loves us immensely and He only wants the best for us. So, tell me how can a loser win? By making God your Source.

CHAPTER 5

As If You've Never Been Hurt

When you hear negative things directed towards you, you must keep moving forward. If you have been abused or wronged in the past, you cannot wear it on your forehead or across your shirt for the world to read. You must keep walking as if you have never been hurt and speak as if you have never been abused. When the enemy gets you behaving like what you have been through, you are letting him know that he has some control in your life.

You cannot live in the past and be consumed by the things you have lost and the people that are no longer in your life. God has a reason, purpose, and a season for all things that we experience in this life. The Lord put you on this earth because He has plan for you and some things for you to accomplish on His behalf. The only way you can accomplish these things is by walking like you have never been hurt.

A man of God from my past who served with me and helped me be a service to God's people did not agree with what God had told me to do. Unfortunately, I could not compromise on this specific situation and he departed from the church. The following week, he confronted me and he said, "My friends and I decided that we are going to sit back and watch you." When he said those words, it felt as if my heart skipped a beat. Just hearing that statement made me feel how Martin Luther King Jr. felt when he was walking in downtown Birmingham, Alabama in April 1963. Imagine him walking down the street and looking around to see men of God watching him fight for them. He could not compromise on the situation because God sent him. Then, realizing that "the battle is not yours, but God's." (2 Chronicles 20:15).

Sometimes it can be hard being spiritual and having peers that are not spiritual. Being an example is not always cool, but walking as if you have never been hurt and receiving your reward is worth it! You must walk it out and not allow your attitude to alter this walk with God. It is easy to do the natural and fleshly thing such as talk negatively about someone that has wronged you or get angry when people disappoint you, but you must realize that you are not in a popularity contest. It is much harder to treat people the way you would like to be treated and turn the other cheek. We are not in this world to please "man." Instead, all our time and energy should be focused on pleasing God. There is no room for natural thinking on this walk.

No one cares who you used to be; the relationship you used to be in; the house you used to live in; the car that got repossessed; how many members you used to have; how much money you used to make. All they care about is the here and now! Walk like you have never been hurt. Scripture says, "The Lord will lift up his countenance upon thee and give thee peace." (Numbers 6:26 KJV). Get peace and walk in the glory of the Lord.

A few years ago the majority of my members were in school or looking for a job. We prayed for jobs and increase every Tuesday night and Sunday service. These members were hurting and did not know if they were going to make it. The Holy Spirit said, "Walk like you have never been hurt." Do you know how hard that is when you are watching people lose their home, car and family? Their electricity and water bills were not being paid.

The Holy Spirit continued to say, "Walk like you never been hurt." Today these same members have purchased homes, the jobless are employed, and the bills are being paid. God is good! Remember I mentioned increase? Everything that was lost has been restored. Now, you can walk like you have never been hurt. Believe that the Lord will take your humility and bless it a hundred-fold.

CHAPTER 6

Your Spiritual Walk

When your walk is spiritual, it is much easier to walk into your purpose. God is constantly providing every step that we take. According to others, favor is not fair. There are many people out there that have tried to do what you are doing with less success. Many years ago, I had service at the housing projects in Fayette, Alabama. My peers told me that they had already tried, but it did not work for them. Just think, how many times have you heard that when you have shared an idea with a friend? Well that ministry in the housing project lasted nine months and every person that participated are all in church and active now.

God had a vision for me and my ministry, so it was time to move. Being led by God, I relocated my ministry to Tuscaloosa, Alabama at The Ramada Inn. Then my peers told me, "Well, everybody trying to start a church." But no one asked me about my vision. They did not know that this was my spiritual walk, not a natural walk. They did not know about the tears

I shed before and after services. When it is a spiritual walk you have no control. You are one with God and he will carry you through. When there is no control you become filled with God's power and courageous in your walk. Sometimes, there would be only one person that showed up, but I preached as if it were a thousand. There was absolutely no shame because it was not my will but the will of God.

I remember the day that I realized my journey was not about the numbers, but it was about my spiritual walk with God. This is the moment that you know without a shadow of a doubt that your mentality has changed. Your conscience will be replaced with an "Impacting the Kingdom" way of thinking. That is when you only think about God's purpose for your life and fulfilling it. Your friends and family will not realize your pain and confusion during this time of transformation and that will make you feel like you are losing the fight. But you will be winning the war.

Now your friends, oh my God, do not be shocked or dismayed when you enter your purpose and your friends have separated from you. They will not understand what God is doing in your life, but it is all for the better. You will change as a whole person, even the things you used to love to do will no longer be in your mind. Your friends will continue doing the same old things, and you will not have any interest. There is a good reason for this: your change will not only affect you, but your friends will be affected as well. They are going to be watching you and be saved by what they see. Imagine that, your fight just turned into a war and you are winning.

Now opposition will start to develop in your family. The family that has always known you notices every change about you. When this change starts to take place in your life, they will be the first ones to antagonize and criticize you searching for your weakness. They know what you used to love to do and do not understand why you do not partake anymore. At that very moment, the Holy Spirit is going to take hold of you and guide you. Your every step is ordered and ordained by God, not by you. We have no control. By your change, watch your family be saved. Something is going to take place in your life that will provide strength for your spiritual walk. When I began my ministry full-time, something happened to me on my job that forced me to stop the madness and take my walk to the next level.

In 2007, I received a phone call from a customer across town. I did not want to go to the customer's house because it was time for lunch. Nonetheless, I was on my way to the customer's house anyway. When I arrived at the residence, I noticed that directly behind the customer's home there was a loft on fire. I ran to the loft, jumping through a fence and realized it was a duplex. Immediately, I called 911 and the dispatcher asked me if there was someone inside and

I said I did not know. I knocked on the door and there was no answer. I shook the door knob and it was unlocked. When I opened the door, a middle-aged lady was laying on the sofa sleeping. I awakened her, told her about the house fire and that she needed to get out. She gathered herself and we left out together. She asked me if I had checked next door and I told her "no". I ran next door and this door was unlocked as well. There was a man on sofa sleeping as well, and this man was paraplegic. I told him about the fire and he stated that the smoke must have knocked him out. When I realized his condition, I panicked. I searched his home and found crutches and a wheelchair. I asked him, "Which one?" because we had to get out of there. He lifted himself into the wheelchair and we got out of there. I got him across the street and the fire department arrived, I disappeared.

On my way, I called my employer and told them about the fence that I had pulled down. He told me to report it to the main office. When I arrived at the office, the safety supervisor asked me to pull my sleeve up and we noticed that the hair on my arm was gone. So, he told me to call it a day and go home. On my drive home, I did not feel alone in my vehicle, it felt as if someone was in the passenger seat. Suddenly, I heard a voice tell me, "If you do not preach, my people will die." I knew at that moment that my preaching and teaching would truly be unique and save lives.

A week later, I started the bible study in Fayette, Alabama teaching about salvation. Years later, I understand the revelation and the significance of that life changing experience with the fire and the doors being unlocked. The fire was my preaching and the people represented life. The Apostle Paul said, "For though I preach the gospel, I have nothing to glory of; for necessity is laid upon me; yea, woe is unto me, if I preach not the gospel" (1 Corinthians 9:16 KJV).

If it is not a spiritual walk, you will give up and quit. That fire showed me, "His word was in mine heart as a burning fire shut in my bones and I was weary with forbearing, and I could not stay." (Jeremiah 20:9 KJV). I could have tried to run, but it would have been impossible. Also, the unlocked doors were spiritual, and they showed me that the Lord allowed this to happen for His purpose and glory.

After the Apostle Peter succeeded Jesus he said, "And I will give unto thee the keys of the kingdom of heaven; and whatsoever thou shalt bind on earth shall be bound in heaven and whatsoever thou shalt loose on earth shall be loosed in heaven." (Matthew 16:19 KJV). Like the Apostle Peter my mentality had to line up with my conscience; in order to be placed into my purpose. This is where motivation from the fire within was created. There is something that will happen in your life that is going to put you into your spiritual walk and change your mentality.

God loves you and He cares about everything that you care about. That statement alone should be motivation enough to thrive here on earth to reach your eternal reward.

CHAPTER 7

Movement

Years later that same motivation made me realize that I was struggling in the process; that I had to maintain my identity, but something was missing. Prayer, fasting and worshipping the Lord started showing me how movement will bring about exposure and exposure would bring about a position to receive what God has in store for me. The Holy Spirit (Fire Within) started showing me Movement – Process – Change. Immediately, I thought about Abram and his movement (Gen 12:1 NIV).

Promises to Abram

12 Now the LORD had said to Abram: "Get out of your country, from your family and from your father's house, to a land that I will show you."

When the Lord told Abram to get out of his country, He was telling him to move. This movement was not about Abram being successful, but it was about him receiving what God had in store for him. In store, meaning that it is already there but you are not able to receive it where you are. If there is movement, not only what is in store for you will be received, but what is in store for those people that you are going to come in contact with will also receive what God has for them. There are people who are depending on your movement. When Abram started moving, God started exposing. God exposed Abram's ability, opportunities, and his enemies.

On May 8, 2018, I met this personal trainer and he was talking about how to fight off different diseases like heart disease and cancer by working out, changing your diet and lifestyle. He talked about how this 70-year-old man went to the doctor and the doctor told him that he was on the verge of having a heart attack and that he had to change his lifestyle. Now, this 70-year-old man is running marathons and working out daily. He took meat, bread and sugar out of his eating habits and used dark beans for his protein. I've listened to personal trainers before, but I was not interested in the intake of protein or cholesterol. All I wanted was a steak every other night, some baked chicken, and I was happy. There was something about this young man that captured my attention, so I continued to listen. Then, out of nowhere, he started putting scripture into his conversation and that really got my attention. He quoted Genesis 1:29 KJV, "And God said, Behold, I have given you every herb bearing seed, which is upon the face of all the earth and every tree, in the which is the fruit of a tree yielding seed: to you it shall be for meat." Yes, he had gotten my attention and I said to myself this is not just a diet, but it is a lifestyle change. It was like meeting this personal trainer was ordained for me. Through him it was like the Spirit was giving me a message to move and immediately I thought of Abram in Genesis Chapter 12. By reading the scripture, I realized that I had already moved. I know I didn't choose Tuscaloosa, Alabama, it just happened. As I was sitting there the Spirit said, "You moved, but you are struggling with the process because after the process comes change." I didn't understand, what change? With no thought, I departed and went straight to the grocery store and picked up some fruit, peas, and corn. The next day on Wednesday May 9, 2018, I was up at 4:30 a.m. working out doing push-ups and sit-ups, and then went to Snow Hinton Park and walked three laps. When I got back to my apartment, I boiled three eggs and went to work. This was my routine for the rest of the month of May. I was on time for work, alert and motivated. Did I mention I was listening to motivational speeches, having devotion for 30 minutes, and reading at least 25 pages of any book that I chose to read? I had this burst of energy to complete everything I started. I called my editor and told her that we needed to complete my book and start making motivational CDs. Through my movement, I realized that I started a lot of stuff and never completed them. Also, I realized that I had not been putting in the work to fulfill my purpose. In other words, I had been cheating myself. I wanted the results, without the grind or effort. The grind is the process, and the process comes before the change. Now, I understand what the revelation of change is about. This is not about the movement, because the movement has already taken place. This was all about the process.

CHAPTER 8

The Process

As I began the process, I started challenging my members to become more disciplined. I wanted them to realize that they needed to pay attention to their health, so they could live longer. I realized that I was more alert and faster on my feet when I was with my customers, and all I did was change my lifestyle. The challenge for me was changing my lifestyle and being consistent with doing the work, which is the meaning of discipline. I realized the thing that was missing in my life was discipline with the things God has given me, much is given much is required. This "Process" had already made a difference in my life, and it was awesome not knowing what else was in store for me.

On May 21, I stopped walking and started running. I thought that I couldn't run anymore, but I defeated my mind and ran 2.5 miles a day. Defeating my mind was my objective every day I got up, because my mind was telling me that I could not do it, it was telling me that I was hurting, and that there was no way that I could keep this up. I was not in competition with anyone, only myself. I started taking this mindset to work, church, and everywhere I went. On Wednesday May 30, 2018, I arrived at Snow Hinton Park at 5:30 am and the Holy Spirit was present. It made me stop and look around the track and It said, "Keep your eyes ahead don't worry about what's behind you, because what's ahead of you is all you need to worry about." That was powerful for me because it exposed what was holding me down, and what was hindering my growth. Disappointments were holding me down, and I was hindering my growth. My ability, my opportunity, and my enemy were exposed. Discipline was needed for a change to manifest. I just existed in the ministry, on my job, and as a father.

I am writing this testimony for you to not only exist, but to change and be a light for Christ. I hear this statement all the time, "It is what it is." I am here to say that is a lie, it is not what it is, and a change is possible. If you take this message in this book and apply it, a change will manifest in front of your eyes. Your family and friends will notice a change. It might be your health, wealth, smile, and most of all your love for Christ, the Author and Perfecter of your faith. Continue to walk with me in this process.

By the month of June, I was treading in my lifestyle change. My friend for the last 15 years showed up to run with me on Wednesday, June 6, 2018. Hey, did I mention he is a deacon of Mt. Moriah Worship Center? We started mixing it up by going to Planet Fitness, working out, and then running. Deacon Banks liked hitting the weights; but running was a challenge for him so we complemented each other. When we went inside Planet Fitness, he wore me out. We left Planet Fitness and went to run around the track at Snow Hinton. My mind was looking for excuses, but I stayed with the plan of Romans 12:2 (NKJV), "And do not be conformed to this world, but be transformed by the renewing of your mind, that you may prove what *is* that good and acceptable and perfect will of God." This "process" has taken me out of this world, in other words out of my comfort zone by renewing my mind to accept the perfect will of God. This "process" is bringing about a position that I had to accept, because it is already in store for me. I have come out of the corner that I have created for myself and eliminated the Spirit of fear. Worrying about what people will say, worrying about if they would accept me if they knew my gifts, worrying about if my lifestyle is lining up with where God is allowing me to go. For me to accept the perfect will of God, I have to be in the right position. Thank God for this process!

For example, there is a difference between high school quarterbacks, college quarterbacks and NFL quarterbacks. High school quarterbacks and college quarterbacks throw the ball at the receiver and their spot after they have run their route. The NFL quarterback throws the ball at the spot because the receiver has proven that he can run routes. The receivers in the NFL are judged by how they get to the spot and the spot is the position. Just like an NFL receiver, I have to find my spot (my position) so I can receive the perfect will of God. This is the scary part of that situation. If you are not in the right position, eventually there will be an interception. The Lord will use someone else to do what He has assigned you to do. Have you ever been watching TPN and heard something that the Lord had given you, or went to a church and your program is working, or you were hesitating to speak about what the Lord had given you and someone stood up and said it? This has been my life for the last 10 years.

CHAPTER 9

Change

noticed in the month of June that I was shifting and getting prepared for my position. My weight was down, I had lost 20 lbs., and I noticed the renewing of my mind as my lifestyle and attitude changed. I started seeing things differently. In my research, entrepreneurs and other successful individuals affirm that you must have the right attitude to succeed in reaching desired goals and outcomes. My attitude started determining my perspective on life because I realized my attitude defined my disposition. I did not know that attitude is 98% of the success formula. I noticed without the right attitude, my gifts and achievements would be useless unless I corrected my perspective of myself and others. I noticed how being healthy drew positive energy and eliminated negative energy. Being optimistic had kept me hopeful, patient, and provided me with the endurance I needed to persevere through difficult times. The right attitude about myself and my life had made me accept challenges as lessons to be learned from. Changing my lifestyle by eating right and working out daily was a process that had exposed some things that I needed to correct so I could fulfill my purpose and get in position.

When you are in the process, you must be consistent and steadily directing and molding. For example, the new millennium child and parent relationship: a parent must be willing to go through the process by learning and communicating with their child to have a meaningful relationship with their child today. A parent must move consistently so they can be accessible at all times until that child is of age to be on their own. All of this was coming to me as I ran in the month of June, and I always ended up with the same answer, "get into position". At the end of June I was talking to Deacon Banks about taking a vacation because I had never been on a vacation.

I had taken days off, but never went on a vacation. I called a travel agent and planned a cruise to the Bahamas. I told some of my friends that I had made travel arrangements and they laughed. I booked the cruise for July 12, 2018, leaving out of Jacksonville, Florida. What a process that was for me! The Spirit was putting me in position to receive what God had in store for me by going on this cruise.

It was the month of July, and I had nothing but some dress pants and a few shirts to fit me. All my suits had to be altered. Progress was obvious, in other words it was bringing about a change. I put in for vacation on my job and my manager asked me what I was going to do. I told him that I was going on a cruise and he laughed and asked, "By yourself"? I never gave that any thought, but I said, "Yes, I'm going by myself." Man, it seemed like the day of departure came fast. Everything that you could expect to go wrong went wrong.

My rental car was not ready, and I had booked it two weeks in advance, but I did finally get a car from a different rental company. Now you know I was ready to throw in the towel, but my friend Deacon Banks was not hearing any of that. He is the one who found the other rental company for me. I departed Tuscaloosa, Alabama around 2 a.m. headed to Jacksonville, Florida. When I arrived in the parking lot in Jacksonville, I reached to get my bible; but I decided to leave it in the car because I did not want to risk leaving it on the cruise. I arrived at my cabin, laid on the bed, and the Spirit of God laid me out. It showed me that the cruise was part of my process for me to get into position. I had been dealing with my communication skills, but the Spirit was letting me know what was already in store. The purpose of my ministry and my absolute love for Jesus was being renewed within me right before my very eyes, what a process! I spent four days reuniting with Jesus. My relationship with Jesus had a new fire and a new meaning. I realized the enemy (myself) tried everything it could to keep me separated from Jesus. When I was in the parking lot talking about leaving the world behind, I noticed how I had stop studying and stop communing with Jesus. Not that I thought I knew everything, it was because the enemy (myself) had me in training camp and dared me to go through this process. Yes, it was literally training camp, and the enemy put me in a closet every day and drilled me about my disappointments. While I was on the cruise, I met so many people and I didn't have to tell them that I was a pastor, they already knew it. I had an awesome time being in the presence of the Lord and allowing my love for the Lord to spread among so many people. The cruise gave me a revelation about relationships pertaining to communication. I continued my routine by getting up early. There was one morning, the Spirit obtained a table for me to watch people come in and go out. I watched how young men did not communicate with their spouse or girlfriend. Also, I noticed when they were eating breakfast or lunch that the men and women did not say more than five words to each other, but they would talk with their kids. For example, one morning I arrived for breakfast and there was a family sitting two tables from me. I noticed that the father was present with three kids ranging from 13 to 16 years old. They were talking and laughing amongst the four of them then, approximately 10 minutes later the mother showed up with her plate and was smiling at the kids. The mother sat for about three minutes and the kids and father got up and left the mother eating by herself. She asked them where they were going, and they shouted, "Back to the room to get ready to hit the pool." The mother graciously ate the rest of her breakfast alone.

The lack of communication between them could not be healthy for the parents' relationship. Later on that day, I ran into the same family and the father was walking behind the mother and the kids. Then, I noticed that the father was looking around like she was his property and dared anyone to look at her. I started writing that nonverbal communication is just as important as verbal communication. I started noticing that some men were walking behind their families looking around to see others respond; while some were holding hands and hugging on their kids and their spouses showing ownership. I thank the Lord for letting me observe this. I started putting together a lesson plan about ownership through verbal and nonverbal communication.

CHAPTER 10

Discipline with a Purpose

I made it back from the cruise refreshed and renewed in the Spirit. On Wednesday, July 18, 2018, my routine started over at 4:30 am, devotion from 5:00 5:30 am, running three miles, and reading at least 25 pages of a book. The whole week while I was running, all I could hear was look ahead and don't worry about what is behind you. It was the same message that I received from the Spirit in May. All I could think of was the Scripture in Hebrews 12:1-3 (NIV) that reads, "Therefore, since we are surrounded by such a great cloud of witnesses, let us throw off everything that hinders and the sin that so easily entangles. And let us run with perseverance the race marked out for us, fixing our eyes on Jesus, the pioneer and perfecter of faith. For the joy set before him he endured the cross, scorning its shame, and sat down at the right hand of the throne of God. Consider him who endured such opposition from sinners, so that you will not grow weary and lose heart." Those scriptures mentioned above were talking about those patriarchs that were overcome with faith in Hebrews 11: 30-40 (NIV). By faith the wall of Jericho came down, by faith the harlot Rahab did not perish, by faith David defeated a lion. By not looking back at those things that defeated me before, allowed me not to give them an opportunity to hinder me again. Perseverance is doing something despite difficulty. I was getting up doing devotion and running without difficulty because I was willing to change my lifestyle by eating right, spending more time in devotion, and working on my gift. That was the movement because I got back on track of running the race that was marked out for me. The process exposed my faith. My ministry started with faith and I lived by faith, so my race is faith. Everything that I have was gained by my faith in God. I came up with a ministry called "Walk like a Millionaire" and it was less about money and more about attitude and belief in the Word of God. Something happened that I didn't realize until this process. This process made me come to the realization that disappointments have influenced me sharing my God-given abilities with others. In other words, my disappointments had turned into fear. Fear discouraged me from going through the process, and from completing anything. I mentioned before that I called my editor to complete my book, but I was just talking a good game. I knew deep down inside that I was hiding my gifts because I was being controlled by fear. Fear took my faith. I grew weary and lost my heart because of disappointments. The race that was marked out for me had become clearer but only if I kept looking ahead toward Jesus, the Pioneer and Perfecter of faith. That is why I kept hearing in the Spirit, "Look ahead and don't worry about what is behind."

By the end of July, the enemy showed up either to slow me down or to stop me, I do not know which one, and it all started with a toothache. I'm very ashamed of this but this process made me realize that I had not been to the doctor for normal check-ups. I went to the dentist and all my wisdom teeth had to come out, and yes at 50 years old I have wisdom teeth. You know things do not bother you until you get them checked out, and man, a tooth ache is no joke. Also, I had a pain on the back of my neck that would not stop. I had the pain before, but I really didn't pay it any attention. I would take an Ibuprofen and it would stop hurting. Now I have had some history of neck pain. Five years ago, I had surgery on my 5-6 vertebras and a plate was put in. Since then, a truck hit me in the back while I was parked at a traffic light on August 23, 2016. I went through physical therapy and I thought I was fine, but the pain would not go away. I continued to run three miles a day even though the pain was there.

I scheduled an appointment to remove my wisdom teeth for September 9, 2018, but my neck was still hurting. I called my doctor and made an appointment for that on August 7 at 3 pm. I arrived at the appointment, and my doctor told me that the strength in my right arm was weak and that she needed to order an MRI. We had to wait 30 days for the MRI, so the doctor gave me some medicine for the pain in my neck and my tooth. I asked her if I could continue to run and she told me that I could for now; but to be careful. I did not know what to think, I did not know my right arm was weak, I thought I was healthy. I had started running, which I thought that I could not do, lost weight, and I loved my lifestyle change. I even started setting deadlines for my book. I openly told my co-workers the date of my book release, and the date of my motivational tape release. I remember the look on their faces when I told them. They never knew what I was doing or that I had the ability to do it. I even had the church working on places for my book signing. I was on the move of completing things that I had started. I told you, the enemy had me in training camp.

Now, here we are in the month of August and the Word from the Lord was the same as it was last month; to keep looking ahead. A form of discipline had developed, and the 4:30 am was my normal routine. My sales were up on my job and the ministry was moving. I had all kinds of personal issues going on, but I stayed focused on my routine. The Lord was working things out for my good, and I was trusting, and believing in Him. It was not that I did not always believe in Him, but this time it was different. The Lord had me to look at things that happened that I prophesied about, so things that were happening was not something I did not know about. Yes, it was different.

On September 19, I had the MRI and on September 20, I heard from my doctor, and the results were something that I did not want to hear. My doctor told me that I had to see a neurologist and that I had to have surgery. In the same breath she told me that I could not have my dental surgery and that it had to be put it off. Furthermore, she told me that I couldn't run anymore. I asked her how serious it was, and she said that if I got bumped or fell that I would be paralyzed. The information made me numb. She continued and said that my appointment with the neurologist would be September 27 at 10 am. I just wondered about how this could be. The first thought I had was that I went to physical therapy in 2016 for six weeks after a truck hit me in the rear while sitting at a traffic light and I could have been paralyzed then. I thought about how while I was getting my neck popped at physical therapy, I could have been paralyzed. I was preaching and jumping up and down, running around the track, lifting weights, and I could have been paralyzed. Then I remembered what the Spirit said to me in the months of May, July and August, "do not look back". I realized that God was preparing me, so I was good and having discipline will pay off. It did not allow the enemy (myself) to bring those negative thoughts into my mind because I had worked hard to renew my mind and change my heart. Through this process I realized that my heart was deceitful and if I would have allowed it, it would have taken me back to my starting point and I could not do that. Also, I realized that I had to practice the word of God, practice loving on people, practice thinking positive, and practice winning. That was the reason for the 4:30 am devotion, reading, and working out so the enemy would not have an opportunity to try to contaminate my growth in Christ. Yes, it was a possibility that I could have been paralyzed, but

God. What was that statement, "It is what it is"? I told you it is a lie, change is possible, BUT GOD. I thank him for the process.

On September 27, I met with the neurologist and he told me what my doctor had already told me. He said that I could wait to have the surgery and come and see him every three months because eventually the strength in my arms would be gone. Then, I would be having the surgery to prevent me from being permanently confined to a wheelchair. My thoughts were only on God's grace and mercy and as I mentioned before, I had to practice thinking positive. I was no longer controlled by fear, so my thoughts were not selfish, and my thinking was not only on myself. The Spirit was telling me to get in my purpose and to get out of my feelings. I had a moment and the Spirit was clear as day. God could have allowed me to be paralyzed two years ago and taken me out of this world. He knew that I could not handle this two years ago, because I was controlled by fear and had a lack of faith in my abilities. As we all know God disciplines the ones He loves in the book of Hebrews and He gives encouragement as a father addresses his son in Hebrews 12:5-6 (NIV); And have you completely forgotten this word of encouragement that addresses you as a father addresses his son? It says: "My son, do not make light of the Lord's discipline, and do not lose heart when he rebukes you, because the Lord disciplines the one he loves, and He chastens everyone he accepts as his son." I know this process was orchestrated by God and that He only chastens everyone He accepts as His son. I had to be reminded of the things that I already knew, because we so quickly forget. Do you find this true in your life? I do. Therefore, when I see another believer struggling, I encourage them with scripture. Sure, they may know that particular scripture, but they may also need to be reminded of it. The author of Hebrews wanted to remind them of the words of wisdom in Proverbs, so they would be able to view their troubles in the proper perspective: "My son, do not reject the discipline of the LORD, or loathe His reproof, For whom the LORD loves He reproves, Even as a father, the son in whom he delights. (Proverbs 3:11-12 NASB). I find the message of these verses to be very clear. We forget that whatever we suffer because of gospel is a sign not of God's neglect but a sign of His love for us. The Apostle Paul said, "For to you it has been granted for Christ's sake, not only to believe in Him, but also to suffer for His sake," (Philippians 1:29 NASB). **"It has been granted"** is the Greek verb *charizomai*, which comes from *charis,* which means: "grace." So *charizomai* is grace. *Vines Expository Dictionary of New Testament Words* says, "*Charizomai* primarily denotes to show favor or kindness as in Galatians 3:18; to give freely, bestow graciously." Paul says that suffering is a grace gift from God. I had to be reminded of the Love the Lord has for me. I could remind others as mentioned above, but this time I had to be reminded of the fire within. All of a sudden I notice the neurologist said he needed a date for the surgery. I noticed I was not even listening to him after he said confined to a wheelchair. I told him that I would do the surgery, and he gave me the days that he could perform it and told me to call and make the appointment. I departed the neurologist's office thinking of the scripture in the book of Hebrews and realized the process of the chastisement of God. The next day I was looking for an excuse not to do the surgery. I was having a bad month on the job, and my personal life was still a mess. I was not prepared to be off work financially, but something came to me that happened to me five years ago. I had surgery on my neck, the 5th and 6th vertebrae and a plate was put in. I noticed at the time leading up to that surgery that my mindset was the same as it was years ago. I was disconnected to my job and my purpose was totally dysfunctional. I traced back and I made a lot of decisions that was a mistake because I did not depend or lean on God, the author and finisher of my faith. During that time, I lost a church, my truck was repossessed, lost my family, and my disappointments did not stop there. Oh my God, this process was awesome, and it gave me the opportunity to see and correct my mistakes. It was telling me that I was running to lose, not to win. This was why I had to be reminded that I was a son of Gods' and that He loves me unconditionally. That is why in the months of May, July and August, the Spirit told me to look ahead and do not worry about what is behind me. God was healing me and taking me to the source for me to dispute and kill the root (Romans 11:16) "For if the first fruit is holy, the lump is also holy; and if the root is holy, so are the branches." Paul's larger point seemed to be that Israel's first fruits were the patriarchs. God set those first Israelites apart as His people. He made them holy in a sense. In that same sense, Paul says, "their holiness will determine the ultimate nature of Israel." That is why she must eventually return to a right relationship with God, which now comes through faith in Christ. The foundation of Mt. Moriah Worship Center is good enough to build upon rather than to start over. The church (Mt. Moriah Worship Center) must return to a right relationship with God, which comes through faith in Christ. The only way the church can make that happen is through the head which is yours truly.

CHAPTER 11

Running to Win

was running the Christian race to lose and not to win because of the effects of disappointments. I know you are wondering who would run a race with anything in mind but winning, who would train all that time expecting to lose, and content to go home empty-handed. I did, spiritually speaking. I observed that there are other Christians that do it all the time. For example: we go to church every Sunday and do not remember the sermon; but we know what the choir sung, what other members were wearing and how we criticized others worshiping. We never take the sermon home and incorporate it into our lives and try to live by it daily, and that is an indication that you are running to lose. Runners for Jesus, remember the goal! Remember the prize! As the writer of Hebrews says, "Let us lay aside every weight, and the sin which so easily ensnares us, and let us run with endurance the race that is set before us" (Hebrew 12:1 NKJV). The process put me back into my purpose, winning the race for the sake of Christ's glory and I just need to run. The Apostle Paul encourages us saying, 'run in such a way that you may win (1 Cor. 9:24 NASB)." He wants us to realize that running just to finish the race will never bring a reward, it takes keeping the goal in mind, and going all out to get it. Just run! I had the surgery on October 24, 2018, and as I gave myself time to heal, the spirit told me to write and tell the story about movement and the process, the change, and how it affected me. So, here I am writing to you. When there is spiritual movement in your life, it will expose your ability, your opportunity, and your enemies. We will go back to the scripture in the book of Genesis 12:1-3 (NIV) when God told Abram to move. The LORD had said to Abram, "Go from your country, your people and your father's household to the land I will show you. "I will make you into a great nation, and I will bless you; I will make your name great, and you will be a blessing. I will bless those who bless you, and whoever curses you I will curse; and all peoples on earth will be blessed through you." First, I want you to notice that it is God speaking to Abram. He told him to go, move from one place to another; travel. God told him to move from his country, his people, and his father's house to a land that He will show him. Abram knew it was a destination, but he did not know to where. Now God told Abram that he was going to make him into a great nation, bless him, make his name great, and he will be a blessing. He told him that those who bless him, they will be blessed, and those who curse him will be cursed, and all people on earth will be blessed through him. Abram did the movement, but the process was the struggle, and after the process the change (the promise). The process is accepting your ability, opportunity, and your enemy. Most of us do not make it through the process because we let our disappointments control us and the burden gets so heavy that we turn back and do what is comfortable for us. I could have turned back and ignored the Fire Within, the promises of God for my life. Instead I choose to run like Abram not knowing my destination. I don't know why it has taken me 10 years to bring out the Fire Within me, and I don't know why the ride has been such a struggle. It reminds me of something LeBron James said after he led the Cavaliers back from a 3-1 deficit to defeat the defending champion Golden State Warriors in Oakland, California with a 93-89 victory in Game 7. Following the dramatic win James collapsed on the floor in tears. He said to ABC's Doris Burke, "I gave everything that I had," James said. "I put my heart and my blood and my sweat and my tears to this game, against all odds. I don't know why we want to take the hardest road. I don't know why the Man above gives me the hardest road, but the Man above doesn't put you in situations that you can't handle. And I just kept that same positive attitude, like, instead of saying,

'Why me?,' just saying, 'This is what He wants me to do.' Cleveland, this is for you."

Against all odds there is Fire Within you. Some roads are harder than others but God would not put you into a situation that you could not handle. I wrote this book so it would not take you 10 years to ignite the fire within you. I pray that this book motivates you to run the race to win, and when disappointments, setbacks, and physical disturbance appear, that it's nothing but an opportunity for you to turn up The Fire.

THE END OF THE JOURNEY

And we know that all things work together for good to those who love God, to those who are the called according to His purpose. (Romans 8: 28 NKJV)

This book is about your discipline with a purpose. God has numbered your days and will fulfill every purpose He has for you. The key to understanding God's purpose for your life is in Psalms 57:2, "I cry out to God Most High, to God who fulfills His purpose for."

Motivation: The Fire Within.

THE AUTHOR

Don Walker is an American writer that has a Bachelor's Degree in Theology/Minister Leadership from Southeastern Bible College in Birmingham, Alabama. He is the founder and lead Pastor of Mt. Moriah Worship Center in Tuscaloosa, Alabama. His heart is to inspire and motivate people into their purpose. His is also a charismatic speaker with tremendous character and motivational power. His Outreach Ministry seeks to illustrate God's love and compassion through action, from feeding, to restoring families.

Printed in the United States
By Bookmasters